D0205024

An Elementary Treatise
Upon the Theory and Practice
of the Art of Dancing

Carlo Blasis

An Elementary Treatise
Upon the Theory and Practice
of the Art of Dancing

BY
CARLO BLASIS

TRANSLATED AND WITH A BIOGRAPHICAL
SKETCH AND FOREWORD BY
MARY STEWART EVANS

DOVER PUBLICATIONS, INC., NEW YORK

International Standard Book Number: 0-486-21592-X

Library of Congress Catalog Card Number: 65-26020

Manufactured in the United States of America

Dover Publications, Inc.
180 Varick Street
New York, N.Y. 10014

CONTENTS

BIOGRAPHICAL SKETCH
AND FOREWORD

Carlo Blasis would have been a conspicuous figure in whatever age or land he had lived. Clearly his spiritual home was Renaissance Italy but I can see him, too, in our own generation, taking the Atlantic in his stride and full advantage of all the mixed blessings modern society has to offer. A versatile artist, steeped in classical scholarship, he was none the less an astute observer of his fellow men and the possessor of a keen analytical mind. We are told by his contemporaries that he was a universal genius and could have won equal recognition as writer, painter or musician. Fate decreed, however, that he should be born in the nineteenth century and that his channel of influence, which during his lifetime spread throughout Europe, should be in the sphere of dancing.

The Blasis family was said to trace its origins to patrician Rome, where under Augustus and Tiberius it was known as the Blassi. Carlo's ancestors distinguished themselves in their country's service and his grandfather was an Admiral who served in his youth under the well-known Carracciolo, a notable adversary of Nelson. Indeed Carlo's father, Francesco Blasis, was the first member of the family to embark upon an artistic career. Destined by family tradition for the Navy, Francesco received his early education at the Italian Naval Academy, but at the age of sixteen he found the life so uncongenial that he determined, in the face of strong parental opposition, to follow his natural bent and study music. His own recollections of youthful frustration and family dissent may well have helped to shape the ideal parent which he was to become. The inclinations and aptitudes of each of his three children were consulted and observed with the utmost care by him before a vocation was chosen, after which no pains were spared to ensure that they received the best possible tuition and the most intelligent guidance and encouragement in their work. As a result he was held in affectionate esteem by them all, as can be seen in the delightful dedication to this volume.

It is believed that Carlo was born in Naples on November 4, 1803 (*see* page xiv). When he was still very young the family moved to Marseilles and it was then they dropped the "de" from their name for political reasons. His father was by this time well established in the musical world and numbered among his circle of friends men of letters, painters and musicians, with the result that Carlo was brought up in an atmosphere very favorable to his artistic development. His eager, enquiring mind was particularly receptive to these influences and assimilated all he saw and heard. His father undertook his son's musical education personally and Carlo was provided with eminent instructors in architecture, drawing, modelling, etc. Geometry was taught him by Ferogio and other mathematics by Wronski. Sabbato de Mauro and later Dutrouille were his tutors in anatomy, whereas his literary studies were in the hands of Guimot. He was placed under the best available dancing masters and since he showed great promise, and a stage career offered the most immediately remunerative prospects, it was decided that he should become a dancer.

At an early age, while his general education must yet have been in progress, he made his first public appearance at the principal theatre in Marseilles. This was followed by a successful tour of provincial towns and some years later he made his debut in Bordeaux as a full-fledged dancer. He had an excellent reception there and the good fortune to come into close contact with Dauberval, then in charge of its Dancing Academy, which at that time maintained a very high artistic standard. In the meanwhile the Blasis family had settled in Bordeaux, where Carlo's father further enhanced his reputation as a composer and held an important municipal musical appointment. His two sisters, Teresa and Virginia, were preparing for stage and operatic careers, respectively, and Carlo himself was already trying his hand at ballet composition in his spare time.

By now his reputation as a dancer was such that he received an invitation to dance before the Royal Academy of Music in Paris and he subsequently achieved a considerable success at the Opera. Jealousy and intrigue, however, interfered with his work there and he was obliged to leave, but not before he had come under the influence of Gardel, whom he held in the highest esteem and who in his turn took a great interest in the young dancer. After a brief provincial tour in northern France, he went to Milan to fulfill an engagement at the Scala, where he danced for fourteen seasons and laid the foundations of his long and distinguished association with this traditional home of opera and ballet.

During this time, he was actively engaged in choreography and he must have been working upon his first book. Here I should like to say how extremely difficult it is to fix exact dates upon Carlo's earlier artistic or private activities. The chief sources of information are contemporary biographers who incline to serve up their hero so heavily garnished in rhetorical bouquets as to make it almost impossible to disentangle such prosaic quantities from the flowery maze. Even the date of his birth seems to me open to doubt, but I shall deal with this later. In any event, we do know that in 1820, when he was probably still in his teens, this Treatise was published in Milan and, by that time, he had danced for at least one season at the Scala and had an impressive number of choreographic efforts to his credit.

The ensuing years brought him engagements in all the principal Italian cities and he again visited France professionally. He also published a book in Paris called *De l'Origine et des Progrès de la Danse Ancienne et Moderne*, which appears to have been a learned dissertation and gained him some recognition in French literary circles. In 1826, Blasis came to London as premier danseur at the King's Theatre, now the Haymarket, where he was given a triumphant reception. He seems to have reciprocated the London audiences' warmth of feeling and he remained in England for some time. He found the atmosphere congenial to his literary work and it was here that he wrote and published in English his magnum opus upon the dance, *The Code of Terpsichore*. Its actual publication in this country was attended by misfortune, since the publisher went bankrupt while it was still printing and the greater part of the impression fell into the hands of his creditors. The result was that only a very limited number of copies, which had already been bound and sent to editors of periodicals for review, were published in England. In the meanwhile a few of these found their way over to France and the work was translated into French under the title *Manuel Complet de la Danse* and ran into several editions. This tome, which became the standard reference book upon the subjects it embraced, covered in great detail the whole field of theoretical and practical dancing, pantomime and ballet composition, with a final section devoted to ballroom dancing.

Early in the eighteen thirties, Blasis accompanied his sister Virginia, by now a celebrated prima donna, to Genoa, where she had an engagement to sing; and while there he met Annunziata Ramaccini, the young dancer who became his wife. Talented and ambitious, Annunziata came from a theatrical family with dancing in its veins. She was ten years younger than he and one can imagine the delight that Blasis took in moulding this promising material into his conception of the complete artist. Under his guidance Annunziata developed into an accomplished character dancer and after their marriage they appeared together with conspicuous success, until an accident to his foot led Blasis to abandon the stage.

This important milestone in Blasis' life occurred in Naples, just after he had signed a five-year agreement to appear at the San Carlo Theatre, and brought his career as a dancer to a full stop. This need not have been the case, as he could still perform all the less spectacular steps, but with characteristic thoroughness Blasis was unprepared to do anything by halves. Behind his joking remark that he would leave the theatre before the theatre left him lay a wealth of worldly wisdom. Whatever natural disappointment he may have felt at abandoning the physically active side of his profession so early in life there could be little doubt that, with his wide knowledge and varied capabilities, he was still upon the threshold of his career. Now he would have more time to devote to choreography and above all to the development of his theories in teaching, which by now he doubtless realized were to be his great contribution to the art he loved. At first his newly found leisure was turned largely to choreographic works composed for Annunziata and it is noteworthy that practically all of Blasis' ballets were pubblished. These, together with his various literary activities, which included frequent articles in current reviews, and his personal contacts with dancers, had made his influence widely felt and paved the way for the assignment which was to follow.

In 1837, Blasis was made Director of the Imperial Academy at Milan, with his wife as co-director. It was one of those all too rare academic appointments that are both fitting and popular. Here was Blasis' great opportunity to put his ideas into practical effect under conditions where they could produce the best results. The Academy, which was connected with the Scala, had then been established about twenty-five years and on the whole had been a disappointment to its governing body. They looked to Blasis for great things and their hopes were well founded. During his directorate it became the leading academy of the world and up to our own time has sent teachers all over the globe to spread the Italian technique. Russia owes much to Italian dancing masters, who have given her dancers that precision and sparkle which, for all their superb native elevation and elasticity, they might otherwise have lacked.

His academic duties did not prevent Blasis from finding time to write and every year saw new publications under his name, ranging from biographical sketches of Garrick and Fuseli to an ambitious work, which he himself regarded as his most important contribution to literature, entitled *L'Uomo, Fisico, Intellettuale e Morale*. Nor did he remain in Italy the entire time. In 1847, during one of the periodic leaves of absence granted to Blasis and his wife, which were of a few months' duration but allowed only one to be absent at a time, he came to London again. Madame Blasis was in the habit of fulfilling dancing engagements during her vacations and Blasis took this occasion to accept an invitation to Drury Lane as Ballet Composer. Later, he went in the same capacity to Covent Garden, recently re-built and re-christened the Royal Italian Opera House. This was his sixth visit to England but sixteen years had elapsed since he had last crossed the Channel and he was deeply impressed by the changes that had taken place. Today we read his panegyric to Victorian industrialism with an indulgent smile. When he ends his letter to an old friend in Milan, "The Englishman is a deep thinker, he has given the world excellent philosophical works together with the steam boat, the railway engine and gas light — so what more could one ask," we glimpse that amusing and highly practical angle of Blasis' psychology which makes us see him at home in an aeroplane or blissfully shooting up forty stories in an American skyscraper.

Taglioni and Blasis were contemporaries but there is little reference in his works to any of the leading names associated in our minds with the Romantic movement in ballet. One is tempted to conclude that his leaning towards classicism led Blasis to look askance at the flood of German moonlight enveloping northern Europe. Indeed, some thrusts at authors turned ballet critics seem aimed at Gautier himself.

To sum up Blasis' achievements, it was his indefatigable industry almost as much as his natural talents that brought him success. Indeed his life was a shining example of his own favorite maxim that a person who knows how to use time always has plenty. The pictures we have of him suggest that he was as robust in body as in mind. In later years, Blasis' personal contacts and direct influence extended to the academies in Warsaw and Moscow and almost until the end of his days he prided himself upon working twelve hours out of the twenty-four. With his death in 1878, a great artistic personality of the nineteenth century passed away.

An Elementary Treatise Upon the Theory and Practice of the Art of Dancing, published in Milan in 1820, is interesting as being Blasis' earliest literary effort and is, in fact, the first comprehensive book on dancing technique, as we understand it today, to appear in print. It formed the basis for his *Code of Terpsichore*, much of the text of which is taken word for word from it. As evidence of its immediate popularity, translations into Italian, Danish, Spanish and English were forthcoming within a few months of its publication. The treatise bears all the hallmarks of immaturity. Eager enthusiasm mixed with the sort of pomposity one associates with a boy smoking his first cigar, only that being Carlo Blasis it causes him no discomfort. The passing smile it evokes from the reader soon gives place to astonishment when Blasis' general knowledge and authoritative expression are compared to those of the average youth of his age. Besides the excellent education which we know he received, his reading must have been very extensive, since he quotes freely from varying sources to establish facts or reinforce his own theories; and if we can trip him up occasionally it only has the reassuring effect of making him more humanly credible.

And there is no doubt that he was extremely human and not always above the tempting practice of a convenient re-arrangement of facts to suit his own purposes. Doubtless, like many others, he came to believe these little flights of fancy himself, as for example the legend that it was he who originated the attitude. His expressed opinion, in this treatise, that the position then in current usage and specifically referred to as the attitude is an adaptation of that which is most admired in the Bologna Mercury, may surprise readers who had always understood that Blasis laid claim to its introduction. So, perhaps, he did in later years, and the fact that he was first to pirouette en attitude strengthened the claim. Then there arises the question of his age, that time-honored test of human veracity. His biographers assert that he was born in 1803, yet in the final chapter of this treatise, published in 1820, he mentions his age at the time of writing as being between twenty-three and twenty-four. Now it seems quite understandable that upon the eve of his literary debut he may have felt additional years would lend weight to his words, but one cannot help thinking that six years would have proved an unconvincingly long leap forward, especially for one already familiar to a considerable public by his appearances on the stage. Therefore the possibility arises that during his forties, when the first biographical sketches of him began to appear, Blasis found it convenient to discard a few years.[1]

But these conjectures, although intriguing, are trivial; the real interest of this treatise lies in its perenniality. It is nearly a hundred and twenty-five years since Blasis wrote it but much of his general criticism is as applicable today as it was then, and with a few minor alterations it could serve as a modern text book. Strides have been made during our own times in the methods of teaching dancing, notably by Cecchetti, who was Blasis' direct artistic descendant, but the fundamentals laid down by Blasis himself are unchanged and the ideals and traditions established by him during his intendancy at the Imperial Academy in Milan find their echo in every well-conducted present-day school of dancing.

Since Diaghilev and his gifted countrymen re-awakened the public's interest in ballet both in England and America, a whole literature upon the subject has sprung up tracing its history and development from Catherine de Médicis to our own times. As Carlo Blasis is one of the strongest and most essential links in this chain he cannot fail, I think, to interest the present generation of dancers and students of the dance. To those among them who may find the monumental character of his

---

[1] Since my arrival in America I have learned from Mr. Walter Toscanini that the date of Blasis' birth is recorded in a Venetian Almanac as being 1797—this exactly tallies with his own version in this treatise.

Code of Terpsichore somewhat forbidding this new translation of his shorter work is offered.

Through the good offices of Mr. Cyril Beaumont I have been fortunate in obtaining a first edition of the treatise and it is from this I have worked. My aim has been to make a free translation, while preserving Blasis' style and the nineteenth-century flavor. I should add that I have re-edited it extensively to spare the reader frequent recourse to foot notes.

                              MARY STEWART EVANS

London

MAÎTRES DE BALLET

Beauchamp—(First maître de ballet at the French
Académie de la Danse, 1661)

|

Louis Pécourt (1653–1729)

|

Louis Dupré (le Grand)

|

Jean Georges Noverre (1727–1810)

|

Dauberval and Gardel

|

Carlo Blasis (1797–1878)

|

Giovanni Lepri

|

Enrico Cecchetti (1850–1928)

C'est en vain qu'aujourd'hui des chants mélodieux
Sur la Scène appellent les Grâces;
Si la danse n'amuse, et ne charme les yeux,
L'ennui suit les plaisirs, et vole sur leurs traces.

FUSELIER.

—— ✿ ——

Today the most melodious songs have failed to woo
The Graces to our stage. Thus, if the dance appeals
To neither wit nor eye, what's to ensue
Save pleasure's flight and ennui lingering at its heels?

FUSELIER.

TRAITÉ

Élémentaire, Théorique et Pratique de l'Art de la Danse

CONTENANT

LES DÉVELOPPEMENS, ET LES DÉMONSTRATIONS
DES PRINCIPES GÉNÉRAUX ET PARTICULIERS, QUI
DOIVENT GUIDER LE DANSEUR.

Par Ch. Blasis

PREMIER DANSEUR.

MILAN, 1820.

Chez Joseph Beati et Antoine Tenenti,
Rue de S. Marguerite (*contr. di S. Margherita*)
N.° 1066.

Imprimerie J. J. Destefanis a S. Zeno, N. 534.

ÉPÎTRE

à Monsieur

F. A. Blasis

mon Père,

CI-DEVANT MEMBRE DU CONSERVATOIRE DE NAPLES,
ET DIRECTEUR DE LA SECTION PHILHARMONIQUE
DE LA SOCIÉTÉ DU MUSÉUM D'INSTRUCTION
PUBLIQUE DE BORDEAUX.

— — — — — —

Des amis qui s'intéressent à mon ouvrage, désiraient que j'en fisse hommage à quelque personne dont le nom servirait à l'honorer. Ils me faisaient même entrevoir qu'un Mécène généreux, en l'acceptant, laisserait quelque gage de plus de sa bienveillance à l'auteur.

LETTER

to

Monsieur F. A. Blasis,

MY FATHER,

former member of The Naples Conservatory and Director of the Philharmonic Section of the Museum of Public Instruction, at Bordeaux.

Among my friends who are interested in this work there are those desirous that I should dedicate it to one whose name would shed distinction upon its pages. They even hint that a generous Maecenas, in accepting the compliment, might bequeath some more practical token of his appreciation upon the author than mere goodwill.

I have considered these assets, which the public invariably appraise at their true value, and upon reflection reached the conclusion that the name of an artist beloved of the Muses, and distinguished for his excellent work, is amply illustrious to adorn the opening pages of a work devoted to the arts! Moreover there can be no doubt that he will be capable of appraising both its shortcomings and its usefulness.

As for the doubtful favors sometimes purchased at the price of sycophancy, I am already the recipient of one so great and granted with such tenderness as to balance all accounts with my Maecenas. I have therefore rejected the suggestions of my friends, whom I thank nevertheless, and have looked into my own heart.

Next to life itself it is to you, revered and loving father, that I owe my education, and although perhaps I did not profit to the extent your pains merited, you are responsible for much of the learning I possess. To your wise counsels I attribute whatsoever good I may have done or spoken, and where is the treasure mortal can bestow upon me equal to that!

Your gift of profound musical understanding, together with your popular lyrical works for the theatre, have placed you in the ranks of those whose memory will remain dear to the friends of art and music. Hence, it is under your name that the public, always so indulgent to your son and pupil, shall receive my work, and this dedication expresses the deep feeling of gratitude, respect and love of

Your affectionate son,

Carlo Blasis

PREFACE

"Song, so natural to man, has always charmed him and in the course of its development suggested gestures related to the familiar sounds. His body began to move, his arms were flung apart and brought together again, his feet followed the rhythm and his facial muscles joined in the movement. All of his being, in fact, responded in posture, step and mood to the sounds he heard. Thus, out of singing was born another form of expression inherent in man, which is known to us to-day as dancing. Such were its primitive origins, and from them it becomes obvious that singing and dancing are as native to man as speech and gesture whence they spring. Since his earliest days to our own time man has sung and danced and it seems probable he will continue to do so until the end of all Creation." (Dizion. *delle Art. e de' Mest. del Griselini.*)

In history we first mèet these sister arts employed devotionally in the temple and the basilica. With the Egyptians, the Greeks, the Romans and even among the Jews, they formed an important part of their religious rites and as time went on they were gradually introduced into festivals and public entertainments. By degrees dancing made its appearance upon the stage and the Greeks interspersed their tragedies and comedies with dances. Their example was followed in Rome and it was in the reign of Augustus that Pylades and Bathyllus, the first exponents of pantomime, delighted Roman audiences with their representations of the heroic and the comic by means of gesture and dance. Trajan banned these fine theatrical productions, but they appeared again long after his day, accompanied unfortunately by the same obscenities that had caused their original suppression; and this time the Christian pontiffs ordered their abolition.

Many centuries were to pass before Bergonzo di Botta revived the ballet in a magnificent fete for the Duke of Milan and his bride, Isabel of Aragon, with such success that his lead was followed throughout Italy. Soon, however, the decline of certain influences in the realm was destined to bring about its eclipse and the Italians lost their interest in this form of entertainment. In France, on the other hand, under Louis XIV the ballet regained all its brilliance, augmented by the pomp and ceremony of a magnificent monarch, ruler of a rich nation insatiate for pleasure. Dazzling spectacles were produced with a glamour and opulence hitherto undreamed of and many of these have since been brought to the height of perfection by the artists who adorn our own era.

The absence of any really valuable literature upon the subject of dancing has led me to publish this treatise. Most of the existing works are by writers who, though able men of letters, have no practical experience of dancing. These are the people to whom Berchoux refers jocundly as

> . . . known for their learning,
> Not dancers, but most voluble about dancing.

The efforts of these gentlemen, who have expended so much midnight oil upon an art of which they know nothing, are quite useless to us. It would be of far greater value if such lyrical fantasies were replaced by a sound treatise on theoretical technique by a Dauberval, a Gardel, a Vestris or some other great master. "I wish," said the wise Montaigne, "that every man would write of what he knows and all he knows thereof."

Possibly the careful study I have devoted to this art, of which I am a practical exponent, and the pains I have taken to make my work useful and interesting will not be altogether without success. Should my hopes be unfulfilled I shall, in any case, have the satisfaction of being the first to document the dancer's art while waiting for a more gifted successor to attain the goal I sought.

Noverre, to whom we are indebted for the revival of the ballet d'action and the art of pantomime, prescribed rules for

miming and laid down certain principles of guidance for composers of ballet. He also dealt with the art of dancing itself, but
his observations were confined to advice upon its lyrical aspects
and a few passing references to its structure. The excellent
letters of this distinguished artist were primarily intended for
composers of ballet, who should never be without them.
Dancers, too, will learn from them the fundamental rules of
drama and simple means of arousing the spectators' interest in
mimed action. But, even had Noverre included technique, or
the contemporaneous attractions of the dance, in his letters, I
doubt if it would be of much practical assistance to us to-day in
view of all the changes that have taken place in our art since
his time.

I venture to hope, therefore, that the following instructions
emanating as they do from the schools of leading masters who
have contributed immensely to the progress and beauty of modern dancing, will be of help to students. Perhaps my enthusiasm allied to my efforts will gain me the public's indulgence
and the gratitude of young dancers for the interest I take in
their progress. I believe, too, that mature artists, used to the
plaudits of the public, will recognize the high esteem in which
I hold their gracious calling when I emphasize how much
charm and brilliance it possesses, and its capacity for still
further perfection if freed from the errors of ignorance and
bad taste that debase it. These are due both to mediocre
dancers and to spectators without real knowledge. In point of
fact, dancing is a difficult art to understand and not everyone is
capable of appreciating it. All too often one sees the public delighted by an indifferent exponent who dazzles them with some
acrobatic antics, whereas a sincere dancer following traditional
rules, yet bringing feeling, intelligence and grace into his
performance, only excites enthusiasm among the discerning
people—unfortunately all too few—who can appreciate his
worth. It would indeed be desirable if the verdict on talent
were confined to persons whose opinions are based upon per-
ception and intelligence and not pronounced by partisans and

the multifarious crew of Midas, those "connoisseurs by hear-say."

The better to achieve my end, which is the production of a good dancer, I have appended to my written instructions some drawings I have had made from my own sketches. They show the positions of the body, arms and legs, and the different poses, attitudes and arabesques. With these before them it will be easy for pupils to understand the theoretical principles that I teach, and in order that their execution shall be perfect I have drawn lines upon the principal positions of these figures which will establish in the pupil's mind the exact way in which to place and present himself in the various attitudes of the dance. Students should study these geometrical lines carefully and note their differences.

Finally, it is impossible to impress too much upon young people preparing to embark upon this art of representation the importance of familiarity with the classical masterpieces of painting and sculpture, as these idealized and immortal off-spring of genius will help to mold their style. A dancer who does not understand how to display his figure can never be regarded as an artist and his performance will fail to arouse interest or give enjoyment.

Chapter I

GENERAL INSTRUCTIONS TO PUPILS

To you young people who are about to take up dancing as a career, and are earnestly resolved to persevere and achieve success, my first advice is to put yourselves into the hands of an experienced master. It is impossible to be too careful in your choice, as by no means have all teachers had a sound training and very few have distinguished themselves as executants. Theory alone does not suffice for the exact demonstrations of the principles of dancing, and far from augmenting the number of good dancers, mediocre instruction reduces it, as everything depends upon the elementary grounding. A bad habit once acquired is almost impossible to eradicate. Even among good teachers there are those with a mania for innovation who claim that their methods are a constructive contribution to the true precepts of the art, whereas in reality they serve only to destroy them.

You will need plenty of courage and tenacity of purpose and I can give you no better counsel than that of a great painter to his pupils: "Nulla dies sine linea." Practice regularly every day and remember that frequent interruption hinders progress and is a loss never regained. On the other hand, excessive work is injurious and may even be prejudicial to health. Be moderate in all things, including your pleasures, and beware of exercise other than dancing. For example, fencing, riding, running, etc., are all forms of exercise harmful to a dancer. Terpsichore is a stern goddess and demands complete sacrifice; hers is not an easy path and you will find many obstacles to surmount. Though you be gifted at birth with the beauty and perfection of form of an Apollo, and every other aspect be ideal, you will never attain success without hard work and intelligent study

7

under a good master. Unceasing endeavor is the price of real ability and even the mature dancer must practice constantly.

You should spare no effort to acquire steadiness and perfect equilibrium. While upon the stage, the dancer should never cease to be a potential model to painter or sculptor and this aim may well represent the summit of his aspiration. The great artist M. Gardel, at the end of an academic discussion on dancing, told me that to judge a good dancer the eye should arrest him, as it were, in mid-air; and if he is found placed in accordance with correct principles, his body presenting an harmonious ensemble worthy of an artist's pencil, then it may be said he has succeeded and deserves to triumph. By this observation M. Gardel shows how deep is his knowledge and how difficult the art of dancing.

The natural ease and facility of your general execution will bear testimony to the mastery you have attained, as the acme of art lies in its concealment. Once you have reached this degree of perfection, universal approbation and the repute of a great artist will be yours. Riccoboni, in his *Representative Art*, says: "Nothing is more dangerous to art than to permit the spectator to penetrate its simulation," and this is an excellent precept for all dancers.

Keen observation and an analytical mind can be of great service to you. Do not scorn any opinion, as occasionally even a poor dancer has certain good points by which you could profit. You should not be afraid to ask your master questions and to discuss your art freely with him. Do not be ashamed if you make mistakes but benefit by his corrections and put his counsel into practice at once to impress it upon your mind.

Worship beauty and never deviate from the true principles of your art. Above all do not allow the temporary success of a few bad dancers, who please a blind public by their acrobatic antics and ridiculous pirouettes, to lead you into emulating their errors. The triumph of these worthless artists is of short duration; truth and sincerity will find them out in the end.

A dancer of talent should have nothing but contempt for the

flattery that fools lavish upon the charlatan and should concern himself only with the opinion of men of artistic discrimination whose approbation can provide a stimulus to the perfection of his work.

You must learn to discriminate between types. Nothing is in more deplorable taste than a tall stately dancer, suitable for serious roles, dancing the rustic's part in a comic ballet, or more ridiculous than a short thick-set dancer rigged out as the hero in an adagio. The ancients themselves provide us with an example of their strictness and shrewdness in such matters by the following thrust. A small actor was taking the part of Hector at Antioch and the audience shouted: "Astyanactem videmus, ubi Hector est?" One of the most illustrious characters of antiquity represented as behaving like a jocular country bumpkin would indeed be a ridiculous sight and an actor or dancer should examine his own physical qualifications before undertaking a part.

Each should have his own appearance and his own fame.
HORACE.

Great artists, whether painters, poets or musicians, have taken care not to confuse the personalities and mannerisms of different characters. They have always adhered to distinction of type and by following them you will give proof of your own good taste.

Interest yourself in dance composition, seeking novelty in enchaînements, figures, attitudes and groups. Dauberval says: "Variety is one of the charms of nature and you cannot continue to please without introducing it into your compositions." Regard yourself as a painter in composing and assembling, to the end that everything in your picture is harmonious and combines a lifelike animation with alluring grace. The music must always be in keeping and it is this delightful ensemble that captures all hearts, and charms even the least musical. Undoubtedly, the pantomime expresses much, but without the tone and feeling of melodious sound it could not move us so deeply.

I shall end my instructions by advising all young students to study both drawing and music, as these will be of the greatest value to them in their art. As draftsmen they will familiarize themselves with graceful and elegant posture and an easy manner of portrayal; as musicians they will possess a surer touch than others; their ear will give them mastery of movement and time and their cadenced steps will be in perfect rhythm with the tune. It will also facilitate composition for those who wish to undertake it and add to its accuracy.

> . . . Terpsichore,[1]
> Euterpe's[2] sweet sister, as Euterpe we praise her,
> She weds her steps to music's dulcet tones
> And shares the self same throne and the same loves.
> Illusion follows in her train, eloquent yet mute,
> She is the versatile interpreter of passions
> Who speaketh to my senses and my soul,
> And in her eyes I see deep stirring visions.
> Behind the subtle mask of allegory
> Are hidden truths, embellished by this veil.
> Rival of history, she tells our eyes its story;
> I see the loves and deeds of other days;
> Led by her, I taste their martial rapture;
> Their exploits cause me wonder and their frailties a sigh.
>   DORAT.

---

[1] The name of this muse who presides over the dance is derived from two Greek words, *terpein*, meaning "gladden," and *choros*, meaning "dance."

[2] The Greek name Euterpe is from *eu* and *terpein*, "good" and "to gladden." This muse presides over music.

Chapter II

STUDY OF THE LEGS

The first essential for the legs is to succeed in turning them fully outward. Strive after suppleness in the hips in order that the thigh movements shall be free and the knees well turned out. This facility will render the performance of développés easy and graceful and can be acquired by regular and intelligent practice. A dancer whose lower limbs are contracted and who is stiff in the hips gains little esteem, as these defects are always apparent in his execution.

By reason of their physique some young people place themselves quite naturally en dehors, their hips are loose and their knees and feet turned outward. This, of course, assists them in their work and enhances their prospects of ultimate success. On the other hand, those whose legs turn inward by nature have little hope of overcoming this physical handicap despite the most arduous efforts. They may attain a certain dexterity with their feet but hips and knees will remain unaltered. In order to avoid disappointment, aspiring dancers should be carefully examined physically before they are allowed to embark upon a career which demands certain natural endowments. Nothing indeed is more delightful to watch than a dancer possessing the good qualities referred to above and displaying a shapely foot with the toes firm and well forced downward.

While practicing take equal pains with both legs, and let neither yield to the other in performance. I like to see them working together in perfect unison, which proves they have both attained mastery. A dancer who dances upon one leg is like a painter who can only draw his figures from one angle, and thus restricted neither could be considered artists.

In your exercises pay great heed to your insteps. Beware of relaxing them, as this is a serious fault comparable to toes that are turned upward or appear ill-matched. Keep their action supple and graceful, strengthening them for movements requiring sprightliness, power and elevation. The action of the instep raises and lowers the heel and of all movements it is the most essential because it maintains the equilibrium of the entire body. By its strength the instep lifts you when you leap and enables you to alight upon your toes. The movement of the knees is inseparable from that of the instep, differing only in that it is incomplete unless the leg is extended and the toes forced downward. The movement of the hips controls that of the knees and insteps and it would be impossible for these latter

The Elementary Positions

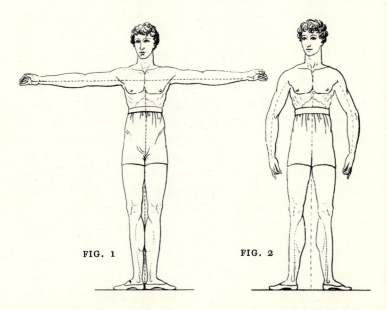

FIG. 1

FIG. 2

In the first position the legs should be quite straight, the heels close together and the two feet completely turned out to form a straight line.

In the second position the legs are separated, but only by the length of the foot.

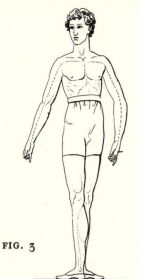

FIG. 3

FIG. 4

In the third position the feet are half crossed and touching one another.

The fourth position is very similar to the third except that the feet are half crossed without touching one another.

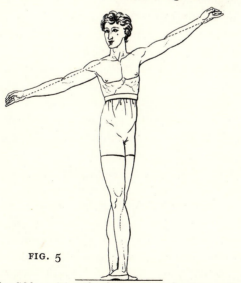

FIG. 5

In the fifth position the feet cross each other entirely.

to move without the hips turning first. There are some steps in which the hips alone move, such as entrechats, battements tendus, etc. Dancers with no natural elevation or who lack muscle in their calves should have compensatory recourse to their insteps. Strength, and moreover sprightliness, can be thus attained but it demands intensive work without a day of slackening. Above all strive to achieve steadiness and precision throughout your dancing.

The bending and unfolding movements of the legs must be easy, smooth and executed with elegance; they should always adhere to academic principles and present a graceful outline in harmony with the position of the body and arms. If a dancer is long in the torso he should lift his legs higher than is usual; this will give the effect of shortening his body, and if he is short in the torso he should always keep his legs below the generally prescribed height.

Many dancers imagine that to be supple and smooth is merely a matter of bending the knee low enough, but they are mistaken; exaggerated flexion only imparts harshness to their dancing. Movements can be as hard and jerky with too much flexion as without any. The reason is obvious when one remembers that the movements of a dancer are entirely dependent upon the time of the music. It is thus evident that if the knee is bent lower than it should be in relation to the music the beat is lost. In order to regain the time spent in exaggerated flexion the extension must be hasty, and this sudden contrast between the two movements gives a harshness as unpleasant and offending as that resulting from stiffness. Smoothness depends partly upon a suitable flexion of the knees but this alone will not suffice. The insteps must act as springs while the loins provide a kind of counterpoise to enable these springs to rise and fall softly in harmonious accord with the whole contour.

Strength and energy are necessary for vigorous steps and temps,[1] but beware lest these qualities degenerate into faults such as rigidity or an unpleasant muscular tension.

[1] Temps is the general name given to any movement of the leg.

A person with knees inclined to be bowed should endeavor to overcome his natural stiffness by constant practice in stretching the knees to render them more supple. He will never make a really successful danseur noble and should take up demi-caractére parts, or better still the rustic style demanding full character dancing. On the other hand, the student with knees naturally too close together should bend them slightly and refrain from keeping them taut, especially when executing strenuous movements and entrechats. There are exceptions to this rule, notably at the finish of a développement, attitude or pose. His physique will lend itself to both serious and demi-caractére parts, and provided he is of suitable height he should be capable of undertaking any style.

Note the following quotation from Noverre: "A person is knock-kneed when his hips are narrow and turned inward, his thighs close to one another and his knees large and firmly pressed together even when his feet are apart, thus forming a rough triangle from knees to feet. His inner ankle bones will be extremely bulky and he will have a very high instep. His Achilles' tendon will not only be slender and under-developed but placed at some distance from the joint.

"The bandy-legged dancer has all the opposite defects, ranging also from hips to feet, with the result that his limbs form a bow shape. Actually his hips are wide and his thighs and knees far apart, so that the daylight, normally seen between certain parts only of the lower extremities when they are

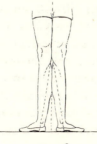

FIG. 6

placed in juxtaposition, appears the whole way down. These people have long flat feet with the outer ankle bone protruding and the Achilles' tendon large and close to the joint.

"Such diametrically opposed defects prove better than any words how harmful lessons suitable to the one would be to the other. The knock-kneed dancer should endeavor to separate the parts that are too close together and the first method is to turn the thighs well outward and, by taking advantage of the free rotation of the femur in the cotyloid socket of the hip bone, to move them in this position. Assisted by this exercise the knees will automatically fall into their proper position. The patella (knee cap), which prevents the knee from bending backward, will fall perpendicularly in the line of the toes, while thighs and legs remain in position describing a straight line and assuring the stability of the trunk. The second remedy is always to keep the knee joints slightly flexed while maintaining an appearance of full extension. This demands time and practice, but once the habit is thoroughly established you will find it impossible to regain your normal faulty position without painful exertion.

"Those who are bandy-legged must concentrate upon bringing the parts that are separated closer together and diminishing the gap which is most marked between the knees. They are as

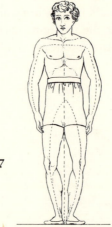

FIG. 7

much in need of exercises that move the thighs outward as the knock-kneed dancer and it is even more difficult for them to conceal their defects. Generally speaking, they are thick-set and strong with the result that they have less muscular flexibility and comparatively little play in their joints. Moreover, it must be understood that should their malformation prove to be a deformity of the bones no amount of work will correct it. I mentioned that knock-kneed dancers should maintain a slight flexion of the knees while dancing and it therefore follows that those who are bandy-legged should keep them very taut and should cross their temps more closely in order that by bringing the limbs together the natural space between them is concealed."

In comparing the two physical types it will be found that generally speaking the knock-kneed dancer is more skillful and has greater delicacy of movement and ease of execution, but lacks the strength with which the bandy-legged dancer is endowed.[2]

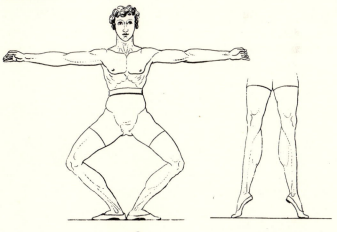

FIG. 8 FIG. 9

[2] In this and subsequent references to bandy-legged or knock-kneed dancers Blasis obviously refers to a tendency towards one or the other defect, as he repeatedly affirms the futility of undertaking the career of a dancer if hampered by any physical disqualifications (Translator's note).

FIG. 10   FIG. 11

FIG. 12   FIG. 13

In all elementary positions one must practice bending the knees without lifting the heel from the ground.

In order to give flexibility and strength to the instep all these positions should be practiced on the toes.

BATTEMENTS

Battements are the movements of one leg in the air while the other supports the body. There are three kinds, viz., grands battements, petits battements and petits battements on the instep.

Grands battements are performed by raising the fully extended leg to the height of the hip (see Figure 10, which also illustrates how the pupil should employ support during practice). After this movement the leg returns to the fifth position, from which it started. Battements may be crossed either in front or behind. Grands battements will help you turn your legs fully outward and render your hips flexible for the evolution and execution of grands temps. Grands battements are performed likewise forward and backward. When forward, the leg should be in the position shown in Figures 11 and 12; when backward, in the position of Figure 13.

Petits battements are performed in the same manner, except that instead of being lifted to the second position in the air the leg is only slightly separated from the supporting leg and the toes remain upon the ground. These battements will render the legs limber, as the pupil is obliged to execute the movement in double time.

In petits battements on the instep, the hip and the knee accomplish the movement. The hip guides the raising of the thigh and the knee's flexion carries out the battement by crossing the lower part of the leg either before or behind the supporting leg. Suppose you are standing upon the left foot and the right leg is in the second position with the pointed toe touching the ground. You must bend the right knee and cross the lower leg in front of the supporting leg, then extend it sideways again. Bend the knee once more, this time crossing behind, extend it sideways again and continue to do several of these battements one after the other. Gradually increase the speed until you can perform them as rapidly as you can count. These battements are very effective in appearance and give sparkle and brilliance to the leg movements. They should also be practiced upon the toes.

RONDS-DE-JAMBE

To commence a rond-de-jambe from the outside take the same position as in commencing the petits battements. Suppose the left leg remains upon the ground; the right one then moves to the second position in preparation. From here it must describe a semi-circle backward bringing the legs into the first position and continuing the sweep until the circle is completed. The movement terminates with the leg back in the place from which it started. This is what we call a rond-de-jambe.

The rond-de-jambe from the inside starts in the same position but the right leg instead of describing the circle backward must do so forward. Later you should practice ronds-de-jambe in the air, keeping the leg which supports the body upon the toes.

At first these exercises should be performed with the hand resting upon something firm, and, throughout, both legs must receive equal attention. After hard practice the same movements should be repeated without support to acquire the erect, steady carriage essential to a good dancer. It is by practice of this sort that one gains strength and the basic requirements for the easy execution of every kind of step. Daily repetition of these exercises is indispensable in order to achieve and retain proficiency.

FIG. 14   FIG. 15

Positions of the legs in arabesques. (N.B. In arabesques and
a number of attitudes the feet should not be fully turned out,
as this would rob the poses of their grace.)

Chapter III

STUDY OF THE BODY

The body should be held erect in a perpendicular line with the legs, except in certain positions, notably arabesques, where one is obliged to lean backward or forward. The position notwithstanding, the body must always rest firmly poised upon the hips. Throw out your chest and hold your waist in, keep your knees springy and brace your back. Noverre says: "Even if one possess all the other essential qualities it is impossible to excel in dancing without being firm in the loins. We constantly see very vigorous dancers who have neither perpendicularity nor steadiness and whose execution is ungainly. On the other hand, we see those who, although lacking natural strength, are solid upon their hips with a firm waist and strong back. In the latter case skill has substituted for nature, as they have had the good fortune to meet with excellent teachers who have pointed out that if the loins are allowed to relax it is impossible to retain perpendicularity, balance or an agreeable outline."

Keep your shoulders down, your head raised and a pleasant expression upon your countenance. In order to give enjoyment to others a dancer should always take an unaffected delight in his own bearing, in the contour of his body, the graceful unfolding of his limbs and the elegance of his poses. The care which he bestows upon cultivating a charming presence will earn him the spectators' gratitude.

A fine carriage is one of the principal merits in a dancer. The upper part of the body should be displayed with elegance and by its contrasts and movements endowed with suppleness and yielding grace, while at the same time rigorously preserving both beauty of pose and purity of line.

The head, breast and shoulders should be adorned and supported by the movements of the arms, toward which they
should incline gracefully to produce an harmonious picture.
The legs would naturally participate in this ensemble, as the
preceding chapter has made clear.

FIG. 16

While dancing, the body must remain quiet and absolutely
steady, but without rigidity, and pliant to follow every movement of the arms and legs. The dancer who jerks his body,
raises his shoulders in reflex action to his legs or bends his back
to facilitate execution is a ridiculous sight. His agonized expression proclaims his exertion and clown is a more apt
designation for him than dancer. I have frequently been a
witness to such discordance and it is usually attributable to a
negligent teacher who, in his haste to see his pupils upon the

stage, relinquishes his supervision long before they have completed their studies. The public, too, by an excess of indulgent applause or sheer ignorance sometimes swells the rabble of acrobatic dancers, who imagine they have reached the pinnacle of their art because

> The mob enraptured gapes
> At tours de force and entrechats!
>   l'Hospital.

These mischievous dancers, whose sole contribution consists in fostering bad taste, should be banished from the theater.

FIG. 17
In arabesques the body departs from the perpendicular
and should be inclined with graceful ease.

FIG. 18   FIG. 19

Attitude derived from fourth position.

Chapter IV

STUDY OF THE ARMS

Perhaps the most difficult part of dancing, and that which demands more painstaking study than any other, is the position, opposition and carriage of the arms. With reference to opposition Noverre says: "The most natural of all the movements in dancing is the opposition or contrast between arms and feet and it receives the least attention. If you watch people walking you will see that when their right foot moves forward their left hand instinctively falls forward. It is upon this natural rule, which teaches us that when the right foot advances the left hand opposes it, that expert dancers base the movements of their arms." I do not feel that this explanation of opposition is quite as lucid as the subject deserves. Moreover it is a constant source of controversy among artists, so let us attempt to clarify it. The opposition of one part of a moving solid to another is the law of equilibrium which divides the forces of gravity. This is what Noverre illustrates in his example of the man walking. Thus when he adds that opposition occurs when the man, or dancer, places the right foot forward, he means to indicate that the left arm should be brought forward at the same moment to balance the declination from the centre of gravity. This also adds immensely to the dancer's grace because uniformity of line is always to be avoided, as all art students are aware.

The artist whose arms are held correctly and moved with grace gives a finished performance which is testimony to his good training. Unfortunately, all too few dancers are conspicuous for the graceful movements of their arms. This is due either to mediocre instruction or their own negligence, which latter leads them to imagine that a brilliant performance with their legs will enable them to dispense with the embellishment of beautiful arms and avoid the hard work entailed in their perfection. These slight artists are mistaken; they will find them-

FIG. 20

selves justly appraised and will serve to swell the ranks of indifferent dancers. Dancing is not confined to the legs, one must dance with the arms and the body as well. "Arms that move gracefully with the body in dancing are like the frame to a picture. If the frame is unsuitable the picture, no matter how beautiful, loses in consequence."

If you have not been gifted by nature with shapely, rounded arms you will have to supply the deficiency by hard work. Carefully considered exercises will enable you to endow lanky arms with elegance and grace and even to disguise their length by artfully curving them. Study the placing of your arms as applied to your individual physique. If you are short you must hold them higher than is the general rule and if tall lower than is usual. A good dancer should undertake every means at his disposal to correct or conceal any constitutional defects that are his, and those aspiring to the front rank must possess this capability.

The arms must always be curved in a manner to conceal the elbow tips, else an angularity will result completely destroying the soft contour and substituting sharp corners, divested of all elegance, for the straight or oblique lines and semi-circular curves.

FIG. 21

FIG. 22

FIG. 23
Incorrect

FIG. 24
Correct

Such position in a dancer offends good taste, and his every position becomes grotesque and the object of ridicule and caricature.

The wrists may be moved either downward or upward. In the downward movement let the wrist bend inward and the hand make a half turn, thus regaining its original position. Care should be taken not to exaggerate the bending of the wrist or it will appear as if broken. In the upward movement the wrist must first be rounded, then allow the hand to rise and make a half turn which will bring it into its original position in relation to the arms.

The elbow also has its downward and upward movement, the difference here being that when the elbows are bent the wrists move with them, which prevents the arms from appearing stiff and adds grace to the action. However, the wrist should never be bent as much as the elbow or it will appear exaggerated. A similar process takes place in the legs, as when the knee is bent it is the instep that completes the movement (in the same manner as do the elbow and wrist, respectively) by raising the foot.

Therefore in the downward movement, at the outset of which the arms are raised, you must bend the elbow and wrist; having bent the arms, you then complete the movement by extending them and allowing them to regain their original position. When the wrists are moved alone they should bend and stretch in the same manner as they would in moving with the elbows. In the upward movement, the hands will be down and the wrists and elbows must rise and form a complete circle, taking care that both arms move in exact relation to one another and return thus to their original position.

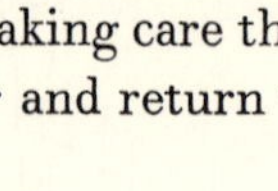

FIG. 25

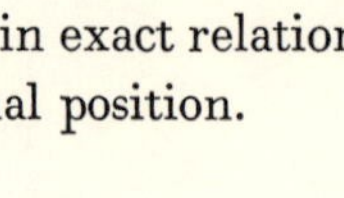

FIG. 26

The small of the arm should be on a level with the palm of the hand, the shoulders low and always motionless, the elbows well supported and the fingers gracefully grouped. It is important that the position and carriage of the arms should appear easy and smooth. Stiffness must be banished, together with any exaggerated movements. Never jerk your arms, as this is a serious defect and the ruin of any dancer, albeit he display the most perfect execution in his legs. (N.B. It should be noted that in arabesques the position of the arms departs from the usual rules and it therefore rests with the dancer's taste and ability to place them gracefully.)

Chapter V

PRINCIPAL POSITIONS
AND THEIR DERIVATIVES

*Preparations and Terminations of Steps and Temps,
Poses, Attitudes, Arabesques, Groups
and Attitudes de Genre.*

Pay great heed to the carriage of your body and of your arms,
whose movements must be soft, graceful and always accordant
with those of your legs. There should be a perfect and unceasing harmony of execution throughout the body.

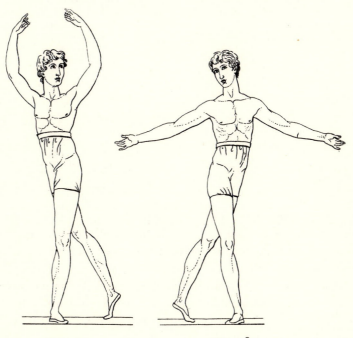

FIG. 27   FIG. 28

Present yourself with style and natural ease even in the simplest pose. Take note that in all poses the body should be épaulé and especially the head, or the effect will be lifeless and insipid (see Chapter III, etc.). In some of the drawings representing the elementary positions of the dance it will be observed that the head is facing directly in front, but these are merely illustrations for exercises.

FIG. 29   FIG. 30

Strive to acquire perfect bodily equilibrium and to achieve this end never deviate from the perpendicular which should extend from the center of the collar bone down to between the ankles of both feet.

If a dancer is to remain balanced upon one leg, or for that matter well poised upon both, he must, besides disposing himself gracefully, establish the correct counterpoise of all other parts of his body.

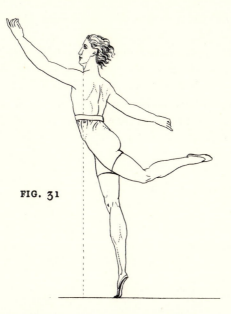

FIG. 31

In this connection the following quotations from an Italian source are noteworthy:

Of the Centre of Gravity of a Standing Man

A man's weight resting upon one leg is evenly distributed over the point that supports him. A man who is moving has his center of gravity exactly in the middle of the leg resting fully upon the ground . . .

Of Equilibrium

A person carrying a weight placed outside the line of his center of gravity must counter balance this by throwing the equivalent in his own weight toward the opposite side in order to establish an equilibrium around the central perpendicular line (see Figure 31).

But in a dancer's position as he springs from the ground, and in certain arabesques where he leans forward (as shown in

Figure 32), the same center of gravity does not obtain (Figure 33).

Infuse your attitudes, arabesques and groups with feeling and expression. The position which dancers specifically refer to as the attitude is the loveliest and most difficult of execution in dancing. In my opinion it is an adaptation of the much admired pose of the celebrated Mercury of Bologna (Figure 34).

FIG. 32

FIG. 33

FIG. 34

A dancer who can dispose himself well in the attitude will be outstanding and give proof that he has acquired a knowledge requisite to his art (Figures 35, 36, 37).

FIG. 36

FIG. 35   FIG. 37

Nothing is more graceful than those charming positions we call arabesques, which have been inspired by the bas-reliefs of antiquity and fragments of Greek painting, as well as by the delightful frescoes from Raphael's drawings in the loggias of the Vatican. Dancers should learn to portray these spirited and lovely effects of sculpture and painting in their own art. It is the fountainhead to which one should always have recourse to mold one's taste in style and purity of line (Figures 38, 39, 40, 41).

FIG. 38

FIG. 39

FIG. 40

FIG. 41

38

The number of poses, attitudes and arabesques is innumerable, as a slight épaulement of the body, an opposition of the arms or a mere movement of the legs, in happy relation to the ensemble, produces unlimited variety. Their graceful execution depends entirely upon the dancer's taste and it is his responsibility to adapt them to the style and character of his dance.

Chapter VI

OF TEMPS, STEPS, ENCHAÎNEMENTS
AND THE ENTRECHAT

Devote yourself to accuracy and precision in your dancing, making certain that your temps[1] conform to the best principles you have been taught and your steps are executed with grace and elegance.

The action in your grands temps must be full, smooth and executed with dignity. The dancer should display great precision throughout and steady self-possession at the conclusion.

In terre-à-terre steps the elasticity of the insteps must be brought into full play and the toes kept firm and well forced downward, as the former contributes grace and the latter sparkle to your performance. The good dancer should introduce light and shade into his steps and by great exactitude emphasize their differences. For example, in poised steps and attitudes he must be pliant and present himself in scrupulous accordance with established artistic principles; where elevation is required he must display masculine vigor, which in turn should find a contrast in the agility of his terre-à-terre steps. But let him always bear in mind that the choice of steps must be suitable both to the style he has adopted and his physique.

Variety and novelty should be the objectives in enchaînements and the artist must study the composition carefully and be guided by his own good taste in its rendering. Never introduce vigorous leaps or exaggerated elevation into an enchaînement of grands temps, and where the sequence is one of lively steps, based upon a brisk musical motif, avoid slackening and

[1] Blasis uses "temps" as the general term for any movement of the leg (Translator's note).

FIG. 42   FIG. 43

chilling it by poses and développements. There are innumerable enchaînements and as each dancer has an individual method of combining and varying his temps and steps he should cultivate his own style. Originality is an ingredient of success without which you will always be a nonentity.

Strength, without stiffness, is required to cross and beat your entrechat freely and crisply. The entrechat is a light, brilliant leap during which the two feet of the dancer cross rapidly and alight in the fifth position or en attitude upon one leg. The latter applies to the entrechat cinq, sept, or neuf, cabrioles, brisés, etc., and also to ronds-de-jambe en l'air, etc. All entrechats that finish upon one leg, as well as ronds-de-jambe en l'air, can be terminated by the attitudes and arabesques illustrated in the plates referred to in the preceding chapter.

The entrechat is generally begun with an assemblé, a coupé or a jeté; the body then springs into the air and the legs pass to the fifth position as they cross. One can beat entrechats quatre, six, huit, dix or even douze. Dancers have been known to press the number up to fourteen, but these are unpleasant tours de force which only evoke astonishment at the muscular strength displayed. The dancer is unable to complete each temps and his body, distorted by the physical effort, presents a painful spectacle. The most elegant entrechats are the entrechat six and six ouvert, the latter accomplished by opening the third temps (see Figure 44), and the entrechat huit.

Other entrechats are the entrechat cinq dessus; cinq dessous; brisé de côté, dessus and dessous; en arrière and en avant; entrechat cinq de côté and en arrière; six battu en avant and six battu en arrière; entrechat quatre on one leg; entrechat sept en avant and en arrière, the cabriole of one or two temps; the Italian cabriole en avant and en arrière; both ronds-de-

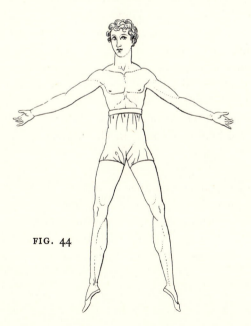

FIG. 44

jambe en dehors and en dedans, etc. All the entrechats can also be executed while turning, except the brisés to which I referred, the entrechats sept en avant, cinq de côté and en arrière and the cabriole.

In the case of the knock-kneed dancer the muscular contraction produced by the exertion of leaping stiffens the joints with the result that all the parts are forced back into their natural position. Thus, the knees turn inward and resume their bulk, which greatly hinders the beating of the entrechat. The closer together the upper part of the legs the more separated the extremities and they can neither beat nor cross, but remain motionless during the action of the knees, which in consequence appear to rub unpleasantly against one another. Since the entrechat is neither cut, beaten, nor crossed at the feet, it lacks the speed and brilliance which constitute its chief merit. The methods of practice which I have outlined in Chapter II, "Study of the Legs," will in time correct these defects. Bow-legged dancers are sinewy, quick and brilliant where strength rather than skill is required. They are sinewy and light owing to the direction of their muscular fasciculus and the thickness and resistance of their articular ligaments, and their speed derives from the fact that they cross more below than above and have much less distance to cover in beating the temps. A brilliant effect is achieved because the light is visible between their legs as they cross and uncross. This effect of light is precisely what may be termed the chiaroscuro of dancing, because without it to give value to the shadows a blurred mass is the result. Bow-legged dancers, however, are rarely skilful because they rely too much upon their strength, which is often in itself a hindrance to grace and suppleness.

Work hard to acquire an easy elevation; this is a great asset in a dancer and essential in movements demanding strength and vigor. Leonardo da Vinci defines a man's action in jumping and the means he employs to lift himself off the ground as follows: "When a man springs into the air his head moves three times as fast as the heel of his foot before the toes

FIG. 45

FIG. 46

FIG. 47

FIG. 48

leave the ground and twice as quickly as his hips. This is because at the same time three angles are obliterated; the highest is where the torso joins the thighs in front, the second where the thighs join the legs at the back of the knee joint and the third is formed in front of the union between the leg and instep." He then shows us how the momentum created by the raising of arms and shoulders pulls the body, already well poised upon the hips and bended knees, upward and raises it from the ground aided by the extension of the knees and elasticity of the insteps. When dancing, once the ascent is accomplished the body must remain absolutely quiet, steady and always gracefully poised.

In entrechats and temps d'élévation one can display nearly all the attitudes and arabesques. Personally I think the most beautiful positions are those shown in Figures 45, 46, 47 and 48.

Entrechats and temps d'élévation where the body is leaning forward are shown in Figures 46 and 48; entrechats and temps d'élévation where the body is leaning backward, in Figure 47.

Be as light as possible, bearing in mind that the public looks for an aerial quality in a dancer and feels dissatisfied when this is lacking. Study ballon; I would like to see you bound with a suppleness and agility which gives me the impression you are barely touching the ground and may at any moment take flight.

If you are animated it will add brilliance to your performance and delight the onlooker.

Chapter VII

PIROUETTES

*Of the manner in which to prepare for and spin them, of
the various positions which can be taken in
turning and of the different ways in
which to terminate them.*

The art of dancing has been brought to such a degree of perfection by Dauberval, Gardel, Vestris and other famous artists
that Noverre himself would marvel. Today dancers possess a re-
finement of style and a charm which was entirely lacking in
previous generations when those beautiful temps of perpendicularity and equilibrium, those lovely attitudes and enchanting
arabesques were still unknown. Brilliance of execution,
variety in steps, enchaînements and pirouettes had not yet
embellished the nascent art and its extreme simplicity im-
posed limitations upon the artist. Nevertheless, it must be
avowed in justice to our predecessors that they were more eminent than we in the grave or serious style, and that Dupré and
Vestris the elder were models in this valuable sphere and have
had few worthy successors. It is true that these dancers lacked
a wide range and a fecundity of steps, but what they did was
done superlatively. Since dancing has become so intricate and
the majority of students devote themselves to all its branches
it is difficult to find a faultless dancer. "He who attempts too
much achieves but little."

We owe pirouettes to the astounding progress of modern
dancing. The dancers of yesterday, as indeed Noverre himself,
were unfamiliar with them and thought it impossible to ex-
ceed three turns upon the instep. Our leading contemporaries
have proved the contrary, and present-day execution of the

47

divers pirouettes is extraordinary for the sustained balance and faultless bodily equilibrium achieved. Young dancers will appreciate my meaning as they know the difficulties, first in learning to balance the body upon one leg, then upon the toes of one foot and finally the hard work entailed before they can turn without a tremor of the body.

Messrs. Gardel and Vestris may be regarded as the inventors of the pirouette, and the latter by perfecting and diversifying them increased their vogue. Other excellent dancers have gone further still and astonishing pirouettes have been performed in almost every possible manner. A pirouette of three to four turns executed in the second position and terminated in the same position, or en attitude, is proof of a dancer's perfect equilibrium and there is nothing more exacting in dancing.

The pirouette requires a great deal of hard work. Pupils whom nature has blessed with a suitable physique will succeed in acquiring a graceful execution, but those whose hips are constricted or who have difficulty in the unfolding movement of the legs will meet with little success. They can only turn upon the instep and must abandon full pirouettes. The dancer of powerful build or who is bow-legged will have the same difficulty, since his muscular strength deprives him of suppleness, flexibility of the legs and the bodily tranquility which is required to maintain a perfect balance. The slender, close-kneed dancer possesses an advantage over the above-mentioned, as he has more softness, more flexibility in his limbs and a greater facility in turning them out. It is essential to be très-en-dehors to become a good pirouetteur, if I may be permitted this dancing academy expression.

In your pirouettes, keep your balance perfect and make sure you are properly placed upon commencing, while you are turning, and at the end. The sole of the foot is the real foundation upon which our whole bodily machine rests. If a sculptor were to support his work upon an unstable base he would invite disaster, as it would collapse and be broken to pieces. For this reason a dancer should make use of all his toes like so many branches, whose expansion upon the ground by increasing the area of support establishes and maintains his bodily equilibrium. If he fails to spread them out and, as it were, grip the stage with them in order to hold erect and firm, a multitude of mishaps will ensue. The foot will lose its normal shape and waver continually to and fro between the big toe and the little one. This rolling movement, which is caused by the convex formation of the extremity of the foot in this position, prevents stability, the ankles falter and the balance is lost.

If you study Figure 49 carefully you will observe that the body must be firm upon the legs in the preparation for a pirouette and the arms ready to give it the momentum required in turning and to act as a pendulum that keeps the whole body balanced as it revolves upon the toes of one foot. Previous to preparing for a pirouette, en dehors or en dedans, the dancer may pause in any of the attitudes or arabesques which terminate an enchaînement; however, the most customary positions

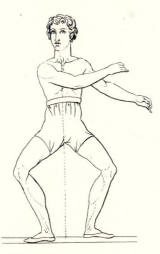

FIG. 49
Position of the dancer while taking pirouettes en dehors. (N.B. The feet should be placed between the second and fourth position.)

and those which facilitate preparation, as the body is already straight and squarely balanced upon the legs, are shown in Figures 3, 5 and 24.

The finish of a pirouette must be steady and self-possessed with the outline of your body and limbs correct and graceful. To obtain the most pleasing effect it is impossible to exaggerate the importance of spinning daintily upon the toe, as nothing is more repellent to watch than a bad dancer who keeps shifting from toe to heel and jerking up and down in each turn of his pirouette.

For the positions and attitudes best known and most generally used in pirouettes: in the second position, see Figure 50; en attitude, see Figure 51; and on the ankle, see Figure 52. One wonders why the majority of dancers limit themselves to these positions, for once they have learned to pirouette, atten-

FIG. 50

FIG. 51

tive work will enable them to do so en arabesque or in any other position. I was the first to depart from the general rule and, having some aptitude, I achieved a certain success in these new pirouettes. The first of these is to spin three times, for example, in the second position and then to place the legs and arms in the position of the arabesque shown in Figure 53, to spin three or four times and stop in this position. If perfectly executed this pirouette is most pleasing and graceful.

I composed another very difficult and effective pirouette in which after spinning in the second position one spins in the position of the arabesque with back turned, shown in Figure 32. The body should be outstretched and leaning well forward with the arms and head in graceful alignment. This pirouette always causes astonishment, as the dancer's body is leaning so

FIG. 52   FIG. 53

far forward that it seems as if he must lose his balance at each turn and there appears to be something miraculous in its successful execution. This is because the position of the body and the arms, and also of the leg which is in the air, combined with the speed in turning, dissembles the center of gravity. Personally, I consider it to be the most difficult pirouette ever performed. I have also spun in the attitude Figure 33 and this is a very showy pirouette. The angular position of the right arm adds sparkle and it is extremely suitable for character dances.

In the role of Mercury, I assumed the attitude of the Bologna statue for my pirouettes (see Figure 34). This fine position is most difficult and unless one is naturally well-set it is impossible to execute the pirouette effectively. The body must lean

FIG. 54
Position of the dancer while taking pirouette en dedans.

well forward and the right arm should be almost fully extended. The leg en attitude should be bent to complete the curved
outline of the pose. To render the effect even more graceful the
left hand, which holds the caduceus, should be outstretched.
By thus eliminating an angle the pirouette becomes more
pleasing.

In concluding this chapter upon pirouettes, I would tell
the pupil that he can turn in any attitude or arabesque pro-
viding the outline of his body and limbs is graceful and easy
and all his movements natural and free from affectation.

Pirouettes can be terminated in all sorts of poses, attitudes
and arabesques. Different types of pirouettes are as follows:
pirouette à petits battements sur le cou de pied; à rond-de-
jambe, in the second position; in the second position with grand
rond-de-jambe; with fouetté; pirouette en attitude and en
arabesque; pirouette sur le cou de pied; pirouette en dedans in
the second position; sur le cou de pied and en attitude; pirouette renversée; compound pirouettes, etc.

Chapter VIII

DANCERS: SERIOUS, DEMI-CARACTÈRE
AND COMIC

The dancer who is destined for serious or heroic roles must possess a fine stature and well-proportioned figure, as this style exacts these physical qualifications. A stature approximating that of Apollo or Antinous in the case of a man or of the Venus of the Troad or Diana in that of a woman would be entirely suitable to serious roles.

While free from affectation one's carriage and demeanor should be stately and elegant. The serious style is the most difficult branch of dancing, demanding an immense amount of work and never fully appreciated save by connoisseurs and people of taste. The artist who gains distinction in this sphere deserves the highest praise and the perfect execution of an adagio is the ne plus ultra of the art. In fact, I regard it as the dancer's touchstone.

It is unfortunate that this beautiful style should now be so neglected, indeed I might say almost obsolete. As has been already pointed out, our predecessors were its masters and have had few followers. The explanation lies in the present-day confusion of styles which is highly detrimental to the art, in a lack of persevering study among dancers and in the corrupted taste of a certain section of the public. I know of only one successful exponent of this style and it is to be hoped that he will never surrender himself to obliging the ignorant element in his audience. The responsibility of re-establishing public taste rests with the artist through the faithful rendering of the true precepts of his art.

A Parisian newspaper referring to my own debut at the Royal Academy of Music in the serious style said: "Curiously

FIG. 55

enough, for a long time the noble and serious dance has been overlooked, in fact it is hard for us to conceive of dancing without gaiety. Yet this solemn style has its peculiar attractions; in it the effects produced by beautiful poses and movements give to the art of dancing an importance approaching that of the sculptor's. This type of entertainment was cultivated and greatly enjoyed by the Greeks and Romans and our present neglect shows how far removed we are from the perfection they had attained. Their mimed play bears some analogy to our own serious dance, which is one reason why we should encourage the very limited number of dancers who devote themselves to this style. Perhaps they have delights in store as yet unknown to us." This last sentence illustrates the complete decline in fine serious dancing when it says that the joys it promises are unknown to present-day spectators.

The serious dancer must have shapely legs, good insteps and great flexibility in the hips, as without these indispensable attributes he will never be successful in the style he has adopted. It is less essential in other styles to possess to a degree the qualities I have enumerated, as the same flawlessness is not expected in demi-caractère or comic parts.

A fine carriage of the upper part of the body, arms that move in complete harmony and the classical finish of his performance should signalize the dancer in serious roles. To him belong the beautiful développés, the grand temps and all the noblest steps in dancing. He should hold the spectator's attention by his elegance of outline and the correctness of his poses, attitudes and arabesques. Within his province come the loveliest pirouettes, spun in the second position, en attitude and upon the instep; also movements of elevation and strength and a fine entrechat. One sees by this that the technical demands upon the serious dancer of today are far greater than in the past and that his qualifications must be many.

The demi-caractère dancer should be of medium height and a slim elegant build. A figure such as Mercury or the Hebe of Canova would be suitable for demi-caractère or mixed roles, and those with the good fortune to possess these physical assets will shine in this delightful style.

The demi-caractère is a blend of different styles in dancing and students who embrace it may make use of all the movements and steps that the art offers. Nevertheless, their manner should always be noble and elegant and their temps d'abandon accompanied by restraint and a pleasing dignity. They should avoid the grands temps of the serious style, as for them unqualified success resides only in steps appropriate to Mercury, Paris, Zephyrus, etc., and in the dances and graceful ways of an elegant troubadour.

The dancer of indifferent stature and strong, thick-set build should devote himself to comic, pastoral or rustic roles.

If allied to this somewhat athletic physique he possesses average height he will also be perfectly suited to character dances, most of which incline to the comic style. In my opinion this style should be an adaptation of those natural movements which constitute what has been known as dancing among all peoples throughout the ages. To imitate and mimic, while dancing, the clumsy gait, the jocular pose and the artless ways of country folk abandoning themselves unreservedly to gaiety and enjoyment is to depict the pastoral style. The pupil setting out to attain this goal should study direct from life and also familiarize himself with the work of those leading painters who have enlivened their canvases with such scenes.

It was in rustic parts and dances that Monsieur Auguste Vestris excelled all others. Nature was his model and he was without rival. There is still no dancer comparable to him and all Frenchmen regret that he has left the theatre. His father

FIG. 56

dubbed him the God of the Dance and said that he knew only three great men in Europe: "Auguste, Frederick the Great and Voltaire."

All dancers of comic roles should study characteristic steps. They must devote themselves to a correct representation of national idiosyncrasies and imbue each step and pose with the style and spirit of the peoples whose dance they are performing. Judgment upon them is somewhat less exacting than that applied to demi-caractère dancers.

The best known character dances are the Provençal, the Bolero, the Tarantella, and the Russian, Scottish, German, Tyrolean, Cossack, etc., national dances. The Chinese gait, clog dancing, the English dance, caricature steps, etc., all belong to low comedy.

FIG. 57

Chapter IX

THE MASTER

The ultimate success of a dancer with a sound academic training resides in his performance upon the stage, and therefore theoretical knowledge of the art alone can never produce an ideal teacher. Only one who has been a first rate dancer himself makes a good master, because in the absence of practical experience instruction becomes a mechanical routine and both lessons and demonstrations lack authenticity. I have had convincing proof of this in my own case. After having been shown the elementary principles, and working for some time at a coryphée's school, my parents, who found me naturally inclined to dancing and wished to accelerate my progress, put me into the hands of the ballet master Monsieur Dutarque. No sooner had I commenced to study under this artist, reared in the leading schools and previously a distinguished premier danseur, than I was obliged to learn everything afresh and forget what little I knew. His methods of instruction were different and the whole art of dancing was changed for me. Its fascination was revealed and although there were fresh difficulties to be surmounted the new method gave me a confidence and a hope and belief that my efforts would not prove fruitless.

A teacher without practical knowledge is incapable of transmitting to the student the true principles of fine execution which lead to artistic success. His misguided pupils will lack the vital quality of their art, and their dancing will be cold, lifeless and without grace. They will present a picture wanting in line and color and with neither light nor shade. As these are as essential to dancing as to painting, their work will be robbed of all interest and charm.

The master who has been an exponent of his art, and whose

methods have gained breadth by long experience, will examine the young pupil first to see whether he is adapted by nature to dancing. Eight years is the best age to commence lessons, as by then the student will readily grasp the demonstrations, and his physical tendencies can be determined sufficiently to render instruction fruitful. At this age, the master should be able to judge whether as the child develops he promises to display an elegant stature and graceful figure, because without these natural gifts, and the resolution to make rapid progress, the pupil will acquire neither skill nor high repute. By my present age, between twenty-three and twenty-four, a dancer should have mastered the technique of his art and be at the zenith of his career. Dancing is most certainly not an art where worth must wait upon years! Equally, we know from experience that a dancer of forty can shine in the front ranks if he has a sound training and is well preserved.

Directly the rough corners have been eliminated by the first exercises, the master should begin teaching his pupil what is known as "the lesson." This consists in the linking together of elementary exercises and the principal steps in dancing, the constant practice of which should make perfect. Pliés in all positions, grands and petits battements, ronds-de-jambe à terre and en l'air and petits battements on the instep comprise the dancer's exercises. In the beginning these are practiced at the bar and later without support. By this means, the pupil acquires equilibrium. Following upon these elementary exercises come simple and composite running steps, coupés in the first position, second position and composite; attitudes, grands ronds-de-jambe; the steps of the chaconne; grands fouettés, facing and while turning; quarter turns, bourrée steps and the preparation for various pirouettes. These classic movements of fine dancing shape the dancer and pave the way to eventual achievement. "The lesson" concludes by spinning pirouettes and the execution of terre-à-terre steps and vigorous movements.

The pupil, however, must set himself a higher goal than

FIG. 58

Example of the composition of groups, attitudes de genres and principal Bacchanalian dance.

that of an efficient rendering of "the lesson." To be a finished dancer he must cast off the atmosphere of the classroom by gaining assurance, and to prove himself past master he must also seek to please and charm. Gracious, easy deportment and expressive dancing proclaim the true artist and win the spectator's delight.

The master's subsequent charge is to indicate to and train his pupils in the style best suited to their propensities, physique and sex. A man's manner of dancing should differ from that of a woman. The pas de vigueur and bold majestic execution of the former is not for the latter, who should shine in graceful supple movements, charming terre-à-terre steps and a becoming voluptuousness and abandon in her poses. Those of fine stature will be directed by the master to the serious style, or danse noble; those of medium height and slender proportions to demi-caractére or mixed roles; and all under average height and of thick-set build will be assigned to the comic style and character dances.

Finally, to create the accomplished artist, the master must infuse his pupil with the spirit, sensibility and enchantment of his art. Should the student have a flair for composition and show imagination the wise master will encourage it by letting him arrange dances and instructing him in design and the beauties of choreography.

A CATALOGUE OF SELECTED DOVER BOOKS
IN ALL FIELDS OF INTEREST

A CATALOGUE OF SELECTED DOVER BOOKS
IN ALL FIELDS OF INTEREST

AMERICA'S OLD MASTERS, James T. Flexner. Four men emerged unexpectedly from provincial 18th century America to leadership in European art: Benjamin West, J. S. Copley, C. R. Peale, Gilbert Stuart. Brilliant coverage of lives and contributions. Revised, 1967 edition. 69 plates. 365pp. of text.
21806-6 Paperbound $3.00

FIRST FLOWERS OF OUR WILDERNESS: AMERICAN PAINTING, THE COLONIAL PERIOD, James T. Flexner. Painters, and regional painting traditions from earliest Colonial times up to the emergence of Copley, West and Peale Sr., Foster, Gustavus Hesselius, Feke, John Smibert and many anonymous painters in the primitive manner. Engaging presentation, with 162 illustrations. xxii + 368pp.
22180-6 Paperbound $3.50

THE LIGHT OF DISTANT SKIES: AMERICAN PAINTING, 1760-1835, James T. Flexner. The great generation of early American painters goes to Europe to learn and to teach: West, Copley, Gilbert Stuart and others. Allston, Trumbull, Morse; also contemporary American painters—primitives, derivatives, academics—who remained in America. 102 illustrations. xiii + 306pp.
22179-2 Paperbound $3.50

A HISTORY OF THE RISE AND PROGRESS OF THE ARTS OF DESIGN IN THE UNITED STATES, William Dunlap. Much the richest mine of information on early American painters, sculptors, architects, engravers, miniaturists, etc. The only source of information for scores of artists, the major primary source for many others. Unabridged reprint of rare original 1834 edition, with new introduction by James T. Flexner, and 394 new illustrations. Edited by Rita Weiss. 6⅝ x 9⅝.
21695-0, 21696-9, 21697-7 Three volumes, Paperbound $15.00

EPOCHS OF CHINESE AND JAPANESE ART, Ernest F. Fenollosa. From primitive Chinese art to the 20th century, thorough history, explanation of every important art period and form, including Japanese woodcuts; main stress on China and Japan, but Tibet, Korea also included. Still unexcelled for its detailed, rich coverage of cultural background, aesthetic elements, diffusion studies, particularly of the historical period. 2nd, 1913 edition. 242 illustrations. lii + 439pp. of text.
20364-6, 20365-4 Two volumes, Paperbound $6.00

THE GENTLE ART OF MAKING ENEMIES, James A. M. Whistler. Greatest wit of his day deflates Oscar Wilde, Ruskin, Swinburne; strikes back at inane critics, exhibitions, art journalism; aesthetics of impressionist revolution in most striking form. Highly readable classic by great painter. Reproduction of edition designed by Whistler. Introduction by Alfred Werner. xxxvi + 334pp.
21875-9 Paperbound $3.00

JOHANN SEBASTIAN BACH, Philipp Spitta. One of the great classics of musicology, this definitive analysis of Bach's music (and life) has never been surpassed. Lucid, nontechnical analyses of hundreds of pieces (30 pages devoted to St. Matthew Passion, 26 to B Minor Mass). Also includes major analysis of 18th-century music. 450 musical examples. 40-page musical supplement. Total of xx + 1799pp.
(EUK) 22278-0, 22279-9 Two volumes, Clothbound $25.00

MOZART AND HIS PIANO CONCERTOS, Cuthbert Girdlestone. The only full-length study of an important area of Mozart's creativity. Provides detailed analyses of all 23 concertos, traces inspirational sources. 417 musical examples. Second edition. 509pp.
21271-8 Paperbound $4.50

THE PERFECT WAGNERITE: A COMMENTARY ON THE NIBLUNG'S RING, George Bernard Shaw. Brilliant and still relevant criticism in remarkable essays on Wagner's Ring cycle, Shaw's ideas on political and social ideology behind the plots, role of Leitmotifs, vocal requisites, etc. Prefaces. xxi + 136pp.
(USO) 21707-8 Paperbound $1.75

DON GIOVANNI, W. A. Mozart. Complete libretto, modern English translation; biographies of composer and librettist; accounts of early performances and critical reaction. Lavishly illustrated. All the material you need to understand and appreciate this great work. Dover Opera Guide and Libretto Series; translated and introduced by Ellen Bleiler. 92 illustrations. 209pp.
21134-7 Paperbound $2.00

BASIC ELECTRICITY, U. S. Bureau of Naval Personel. Originally a training course, best non-technical coverage of basic theory of electricity and its applications. Fundamental concepts, batteries, circuits, conductors and wiring techniques, AC and DC, inductance and capacitance, generators, motors, transformers, magnetic amplifiers, synchros, servomechanisms, etc. Also covers blue-prints, electrical diagrams, etc. Many questions, with answers. 349 illustrations. x + 448pp. 6½ x 9¼.
20973-3 Paperbound $3.50

REPRODUCTION OF SOUND, Edgar Villchur. Thorough coverage for laymen of high fidelity systems, reproducing systems in general, needles, amplifiers, preamps, loudspeakers, feedback, explaining physical background. "A rare talent for making technicalities vividly comprehensible," R. Darrell, *High Fidelity.* 69 figures. iv + 92pp.
21515-6 Paperbound $1.35

HEAR ME TALKIN' TO YA: THE STORY OF JAZZ AS TOLD BY THE MEN WHO MADE IT, Nat Shapiro and Nat Hentoff. Louis Armstrong, Fats Waller, Jo Jones, Clarence Williams, Billy Holiday, Duke Ellington, Jelly Roll Morton and dozens of other jazz greats tell how it was in Chicago's South Side, New Orleans, depression Harlem and the modern West Coast as jazz was born and grew. xvi + 429pp.
21726-4 Paperbound $3.95

FABLES OF AESOP, translated by Sir Roger L'Estrange. A reproduction of the very rare 1931 Paris edition; a selection of the most interesting fables, together with 50 imaginative drawings by Alexander Calder. v + 128pp. 6½x9¼.
21780-9 Paperbound $1.50

DESIGN BY ACCIDENT; A BOOK OF "ACCIDENTAL EFFECTS" FOR ARTISTS AND DESIGNERS, James F. O'Brien. Create your own unique, striking, imaginative effects by "controlled accident" interaction of materials: paints and lacquers, oil and water based paints, splatter, crackling materials, shatter, similar items. Everything you do will be different; first book on this limitless art, so useful to both fine artist and commercial artist. Full instructions. 192 plates showing "accidents," 8 in color. viii + 215pp. 8⅜ x 11¼. 21942-9 Paperbound $3.75

THE BOOK OF SIGNS, Rudolf Koch. Famed German type designer draws 493 beautiful symbols: religious, mystical, alchemical, imperial, property marks, runes, etc. Remarkable fusion of traditional and modern. Good for suggestions of timelessness, smartness, modernity. Text. vi + 104pp. 6⅛ x 9¼. 20162-7 Paperbound $1.50

HISTORY OF INDIAN AND INDONESIAN ART, Ananda K. Coomaraswamy. An unabridged republication of one of the finest books by a great scholar in Eastern art. Rich in descriptive material, history, social backgrounds; Sunga reliefs, Rajput paintings, Gupta temples, Burmese frescoes, textiles, jewelry, sculpture, etc. 400 photos. viii + 423pp. 6⅜ x 9¾. 21436-2 Paperbound $5.00

PRIMITIVE ART, Franz Boas. America's foremost anthropologist surveys textiles, ceramics, woodcarving, basketry, metalwork, etc.; patterns, technology, creation of symbols, style origins. All areas of world, but very full on Northwest Coast Indians. More than 350 illustrations of baskets, boxes, totem poles, weapons, etc. 378 pp. 20025-6 Paperbound $3.00

THE GENTLEMAN AND CABINET MAKER'S DIRECTOR, Thomas Chippendale. Full reprint (third edition, 1762) of most influential furniture book of all time, by master cabinetmaker. 200 plates, illustrating chairs, sofas, mirrors, tables, cabinets, plus 24 photographs of surviving pieces. Biographical introduction by N. Bienenstock. vi + 249pp. 9⅞ x 12¾. 21601-2 Paperbound $5.00

AMERICAN ANTIQUE FURNITURE, Edgar G. Miller, Jr. The basic coverage of all American furniture before 1840. Individual chapters cover type of furniture—clocks, tables, sideboards, etc.—chronologically, with inexhaustible wealth of data. More than 2100 photographs, all identified, commented on. Essential to all early American collectors. Introduction by H. E. Keyes. vi + 1106pp. 7⅞ x 10¾. 21599-7, 21600-4 Two volumes, Paperbound $11.00

PENNSYLVANIA DUTCH AMERICAN FOLK ART, Henry J. Kauffman. 279 photos, 28 drawings of tulipware, Fraktur script, painted tinware, toys, flowered furniture, quilts, samplers, hex signs, house interiors, etc. Full descriptive text. Excellent for tourist, rewarding for designer, collector. Map. 146pp. 7⅞ x 10¾. 21205-X Paperbound $3.00

EARLY NEW ENGLAND GRAVESTONE RUBBINGS, Edmund V. Gillon, Jr. 43 photographs, 226 carefully reproduced rubbings show heavily symbolic, sometimes macabre early gravestones, up to early 19th century. Remarkable early American primitive art, occasionally strikingly beautiful; always powerful. Text. xxvi + 207pp. 8⅜ x 11¼. 21380-3 Paperbound $4.00

MATHEMATICAL PUZZLES FOR BEGINNERS AND ENTHUSIASTS, Geoffrey Mott-Smith. 189 puzzles from easy to difficult—involving arithmetic, logic, algebra, properties of digits, probability, etc.—for enjoyment and mental stimulus. Explanation of mathematical principles behind the puzzles. 135 illustrations. viii + 248pp.
20198-8 Paperbound $2.00

PAPER FOLDING FOR BEGINNERS, William D. Murray and Francis J. Rigney. Easiest book on the market, clearest instructions on making interesting, beautiful origami. Sail boats, cups, roosters, frogs that move legs, bonbon boxes, standing birds, etc. 40 projects; more than 275 diagrams and photographs. 94pp.
20713-7 Paperbound $1.00

TRICKS AND GAMES ON THE POOL TABLE, Fred Herrmann. 79 tricks and games— some solitaires, some for two or more players, some competitive games—to entertain you between formal games. Mystifying shots and throws, unusual caroms, tricks involving such props as cork, coins, a hat, etc. Formerly *Fun on the Pool Table*. 77 figures. 95pp.
21814-7 Paperbound $1.25

HAND SHADOWS TO BE THROWN UPON THE WALL: A SERIES OF NOVEL AND AMUSING FIGURES FORMED BY THE HAND, Henry Bursill. Delightful picturebook from great-grandfather's day shows how to make 18 different hand shadows: a bird that flies, duck that quacks, dog that wags his tail, camel, goose, deer, boy, turtle, etc. Only book of its sort. vi + 33pp. 6½ x 9¼. 21779-5 Paperbound $1.00

WHITTLING AND WOODCARVING, E. J. Tangerman. 18th printing of best book on market. "If you can cut a potato you can carve" toys and puzzles, chains, chessmen, caricatures, masks, frames, woodcut blocks, surface patterns, much more. Information on tools, woods, techniques. Also goes into serious wood sculpture from Middle Ages to present, East and West. 464 photos, figures. x + 293pp.
20965-2 Paperbound $2.50

HISTORY OF PHILOSOPHY, Julián Marias. Possibly the clearest, most easily followed, best planned, most useful one-volume history of philosophy on the market; neither skimpy nor overfull. Full details on system of every major philosopher and dozens of less important thinkers from pre-Socratics up to Existentialism and later. Strong on many European figures usually omitted. Has gone through dozens of editions in Europe. 1966 edition, translated by Stanley Appelbaum and Clarence Strowbridge. xviii + 505pp. 21739-6 Paperbound $3.50

YOGA: A SCIENTIFIC EVALUATION, Kovoor T. Behanan. Scientific but non-technical study of physiological results of yoga exercises; done under auspices of Yale U. Relations to Indian thought, to psychoanalysis, etc. 16 photos. xxiii + 270pp.
20505-3 Paperbound $2.50

Prices subject to change without notice.
Available at your book dealer or write for free catalogue to Dept. GI, Dover Publications, Inc., 180 Varick St., N. Y., N. Y. 10014. Dover publishes more than 150 books each year on science, elementary and advanced mathematics, biology, music, art, literary history, social sciences and other areas.